When God Says

NOTHING

DISCOVERING POWERFUL KEYS TO ANSWERED PRAYER WHEN GOD IS NOT ANSWERING

by

John Utley

When God Says Nothing

© 2010 by John Utley
P.O. Box 840
Granger, IN 46530

Cover Design by Jonathan Utley

Photo of John Utley, courtesy of Alycia Weaver; Sunrise
Cover Photo courtesy of Joanna Utley-Fredere

Italics in Scripture quotations are the author's emphasis.

Scripture is from *The Holy Bible,* New International Version
(NIV)© 1973, 1984 by International Bible Society, used by
permission of Zondervan Publishing House, Grand Rapids, MI
49530. All rights reserved.

Scripture quotations marked (NLT) are taken from the Holy
Bible, New Living Translation, copyright © 1996, 2004, 2007. Used
by permission of Tyndale House Publishers, Inc., Carol Stream,
Illinois 60188. All rights reserved.

Printed in the United States of America

My deepest appreciation to.....

My wife, Susan, who is my best friend. You are a virtuous woman, filled with life and love. Every day I give thanks to God for blessing me with the best wife that any man could want or hope for and I love you deeply!

My daughter, Joanna (who selflessly edited the book), her new husband, Bobby (we are so thankful for you), my son, Jonathan (who designed the cover) and Joshua (who encouraged me). I cannot express to each of you how proud I am of each of you. You bring me joy every day! I love you all.

My family and friends who encourage me daily. If I were to name each one, it would fill this book many times over.

Most importantly, Praise be to the God and Father of our Lord Jesus Christ, who has blessed us in the heavenly realms with every spiritual blessing in Christ. (Ephesians 1:3, NLT) My sincere thanks to our heavenly Father for His indescribable gift, for our Lord Jesus Christ for His undying love for me, and the Holy Spirit who guides me daily.

4

CONTENTS

INTRODUCTION

Tears streamed down her cheeks as she shared her frustration and fear. Her home was about to be foreclosed, she had already lost one of her vehicles to repossession and the business that she believed would provide a great retirement had long since shut down. She was at the end of her rope, her sanity, and her faith. In the midst of her tears and fears, the one thing that caused the most concern was the silence from heaven.

Powerful silence. Earth-shattering silence.

She was not a novice of prayer, or a new believer. She had called on God many times and had seen God answer mightily repeatedly. Before, when God answered, generally a powerful miracle was hers, for she knew how to touch God. She had experienced the power of God and had heard the still small voice of God in her spirit many times. This time, though, she did not understand the reluctance of God to answer her cry, or to speak to her spirit.

She wondered aloud if God had forgotten her, or if God was angry with her.

She looked into my eyes and asked me, "Pastor John, what do I do when I pray but God says nothing?" It is for her, and for so many people of prayer that this book is dedicated. What do you do "WHEN GOD SAYS NOTHING"? What do you do with a silent heaven? When you pray and pray for help and the only thing you hear in return are the ambient sounds of nothing. This is not "Blessed Quietness" but the hardest trial of the believing, prayer warrior: Silent Majesty!

But that silence can give way to the greatest spiritual experience you have ever had, and could possibly open the door to miracles, including the very one you have prayed so long to see come to pass.

1

Praying Fervently!

Have you ever prayed for a need that went unanswered? Have you wondered if God was listening, or even if He cared? Have you prayed with great passion only to find heaven silent to your cry? Have you ever wondered why?

You may have prayed with great passion, for a need that was very dear to your life, only to feel as if the ceilings were brass, and every prayer you prayed bounced back off that ceiling. During those times of prayer, it is not only important *what you pray*, but also what you do with the feeling that God does not hear. What follows your time of praying to a silent heaven will dictate whether you see victory in your need, or else go away disappointed with an unmet need. It is not only *what you say* in praying that matters, but also *what you do* afterward.

I was serving in a small-town church as a young pastor when I received a call from a desperate member. Little did I know that call would significantly alter my view of faith. The phone rang and the woman at the other end could not hide her desperation. She had suffered from a chronic disease for many years. When the doctor told her that she had this condition, she faced her disease with fear as she had witnessed the pain and suffering others had endured with the same condition. Fortunately for her, she knew what to do with her problem. She took her need to God in prayer.

She certainly did not have the answer but she had personally experienced the healing power of God in her life through the years. She knew God and served Him faithfully. It would seem to be a given: She was faithful, and God would heal her. Many evangelists and pastors with known healing ministries had prayed for her. Tapes and books testifying of God's healing power filled her house. Now, the questions were pouring through her lips. She had prayed, but wondered if God was listening.

With that question, I began to retrace spiritual steps I had taken in my life. Those steps led me back to a small church in Arkansas where Pastor Kevin Orr challenged me to go to a deep level in God. It was a time where I would come face to face with Deity and my life would never be the same again. Those steps were defining steps in my walk with God. Then and now, I believed that God was passionate about the relationship I had with Him. I felt that God really wanted me to know Him, to serve Him and, through prayer, talk to Him. Prayer would become the step that would take me to deeper levels in God. From that time, I developed a personal theology of prayer. Not that I had any theological training, nor any great depth in biblical study, I only had a simple faith.

Faith is what I call it today, although I know the depth of faith is not in simply believing God, but in trusting God when I do not know why. My prayer theology included praying for requests, believing that God had what was needed in the situation and the matter was settled. "God said it; I believed it and that settled it" was the bumper sticker faith I had then! So my prayer was simply, "God I need... God you can...

and I believe you will." I would complete my prayer time with a confidence that asking God was sufficient for the need to be met.

This is not a bad way to live. God wants us to have faith. Not the ethereal faith proposed in the world today, but a genuine faith that transcends problems and touches God. God requires this kind of faith:

"And without faith it is impossible to please God, because anyone who comes to him must believe that he exists and that he rewards those who earnestly seek him. Hebrews 11:6 (NIV)

However, something began happening that changed my perspective of unanswered prayer. It began with a promise God gave, spoken to me and into my life that I truly believed He would fulfill. The realization to God's promise has not occurred, and the longer I have lived, the more distant that promise has become. The prayers I have prayed in pursuit of that promise for many years seem to have been ignored. That has not always been the case.

I have prayed for things or situations and immediately God undertook and an answer came.

Nothing builds your faith as those times! When you pray, sometimes God answers immediately.

It is not always that way, though. Sometimes, the prayer times we experience are not fraught with the answers we want. Sometimes our requests do not net us the answers we feel we need. What do we do when those times come, or even when there is no answer at all?

Sometimes God says "yes"

Most all of my prayers have been answered in some way. Sometimes I pray and God says yes. I remember a deaf woman in Quito, Ecuador who, after a group of believers prayed for her, God restored her hearing. When God's people prayed the prayer of faith for her, God answered and now she can hear the sweet sound of her grandchildren. Another instance happened when my wife Susan and I prayed for a home to call our very own, God moved within hours to make provision for us.

Elijah was a man of great prayer answers. He prayed and the rain stopped. He prayed and the fire fell. He prayed and the rain came. James gives us a glimpse into this man of power prayer:

"The prayer of a righteous man is powerful and effective. Elijah was a man just like us. He prayed earnestly that it would not rain, and it did not rain on the land for three and a half years. Again he prayed, and the heavens gave rain, and the earth produced its crops." James 5:16b-18 (NIV)

There are times we have Elijah-like answers to our powerful prayers. We pray; God answers. Sometimes it is right away. Those are significant faith building times. Those times give us confidence that God is a prayer answering God. We become more convinced that God is:

"...able to do immeasurably more than all we ask or imagine, according to his power that is at work within us," Eph 3:20 (NIV)

Blind Bartemaus knows about quick answers to prayer. He asked, and immediately Jesus answered. For a blind man this was a defining moment in his life.

He met the Master, and gained sight for the first time in his life.

Joshua also found immediate answer to seeking God's face when he was leading the children of Israel into the Promised Land. Some answers are a given. We pray and since God has already made provision, the answer is immediate and "yes".

When God says yes to our prayers, it gives us prayer energy. It motivates us to pray the more. It helps us to realize that God wants a relationship with us and that He is able to do the amazing. It gives rise to praise.

Sometimes he says "yes"... sometimes "wait"...

Sometimes God says wait. Maybe the timing is wrong. Maybe the circumstances are not right. Maybe the players in our prayers are not in place. It is not a prayer out of God's perfect will; it is a prayer out of God's perfect timing. Although our God transcends time and eternity, He is very precise in His timing...

"But when the time had fully come, God sent his Son, born of a woman, born under law," Gal 4:4 (NIV)

Maybe you do not have an answer because the time is not right. Waiting is a faith exercise. This is where patience and trust are tested to the highest degree.

This is where the plans of God, perfect and wonderful plans, meet our finite knowledge of the need or the time needed for full provision to be met.

"For I know the plans I have for you," declares the LORD, "plans to prosper you and not to harm you, plans to give you hope and a future." Jeremiah 29:11 (NIV)

Timing is key to our God. Timing will come to play when Jesus returns for the church. Timing plays into when God's grand plans for a people materialize.

Sometimes God does not say yes, he says hold on.

Sometimes God says "yes," sometimes "not yet," sometimes "no"...

Some things I have prayed for have garnered another response. God said, "No!" Not yes; not wait; but a solid: No! I cannot say I have always enjoyed those moments when God said "NO."

David's Answer was NO!

David experienced a time when God said "No." David had such a passion for God that He desired to build a permanent place of worship for Israel. A place where people would no longer wander about, but an entire nation could come together at one place for worship. He developed the plans, raised the funds, and shared his grand vision with many to construct a temple for the Lord.

The prophet Nathan heard the vision and initially told David to get to the work at hand. It sounded like a God given dream. Everyone was excited and David affirmed. That night, however, the Lord spoke to Nathan. God told the prophet that the dream to build the temple was not for David, but for Solomon to complete. God, in essence, told David,

> Psalm 23 remains and has stood the test of time while the temple David longed to build has long since been destroyed.

"No"! Many would say that David was the perfect choice to build the temple. After all, he brought the ark to Jerusalem, he was a man after God's own heart, and he was the writer of so much worship that he had to be the man! However, God said no.

For David, this must have been disheartening. He loved God and desired to please God. It is interesting to note however, that though David did not build the temple as his heart desired, his writings have survived for thousands of years. Psalms 23 has stood the test of time and trials for untold millions. It has remained a beacon of hope for those needing to know God cares. It remains, but the temple that Solomon built is destroyed.

Sometimes we feel God has forsaken us when He says "no" to our request. It may be that God has a far greater plan, one that will stand the test of time, while our request is for an immediate fix. One will last; the other will fade away quickly.

Paul's Answer was NO!

Paul was also the recipient of the answer of "NO". Paul prayed three times for a difficulty he was facing. He called it a "thorn in the flesh". While we do not know what it was, we can all testify to times that we carry some burden, face some trial, endure some pain, and pray for God to take it away. Paul did, but God said "no." Nevertheless, a special provision was there for Paul: "My grace will sustain you!" God promised.

Sometimes when God says no, he provides no immediate reason but He usually provides the grace to go on. We do not always know the reason God tells us "no" to a request right away. We trudge on, wondering why. However, eventually, God will reveal His grand purpose for our life.

Prayers that are legitimately outside the will of God, revealed in His word, will be answered the same way: NO! Expressly spoken, or not, obedience to God's known will (the Bible) is vital to your walk with God, and your answered prayer.

The Bible expresses God's known will, every single time.

That is not saying you will not get your way. You may pray for something God has expressly written is against His will, and you may get what you have asked for, but that does not mean God answered you with agreement to your disobedience. Search the Bible for answers and pray for His will to be done in your life. If His word (the Bible) says something is wrong, do not pray for it.

Most every praying, believing Christian has experienced each of these responses from God. Any praying person can testify of "yes" answers, "wait" answers, and "no" answers. But these <u>ARE</u> answers. He has spoken through His word, through circumstances or possibly through His still small prompting and we can rejoice over answered prayer. For even answers of "NO" or "WAIT" <u>are</u> answers.

What happens when God says nothing?

You pray, seek God, plead, intercede and the heavens are silent. God is not saying anything. How can you find an answer to your prayer when the one you are seeking is silent?

He is not saying "yes," not "wait," not "no,"

He is saying nothing!

If you are praying about a need and it seems as if God is saying nothing, you are in good company.

There are times when we pray for a legitimate need, with as much passion as we can muster, but He says nothing in return.

One of my favorite passages is found in Matthew 15:

> "Leaving that place, Jesus withdrew to the region of Tyre and Sidon. A Canaanite woman from that vicinity came to him, crying out, "Lord, Son of David, have mercy on me! My daughter is suffering terribly from demon-possession." Matt 15:21-23 (NIV)

This Canaanite woman had a great need. No doubt, her daughter had suffered for a number of years. This mother had endured the midnight screams and the fear that her daughter would suffer from demon possession for the rest of her life. No doubt, she had wondered why her daughter did not play or respond like all other girls her age. She probably had tried a number of methods to see her daughter come to wholeness and freedom from this possession of the demonic spirit. She had great reason to come to Jesus. She had heard the stories about Him. She knew her hope was standing in front of her. She responded in light of her situation with faith.

I have not had children suffering with demonic possession. However, I have had needs that were very serious. And, like this woman, I sought the Lord with faith. Her need was great, and she had endured numerous years enduring her situation. It would be easy to overlook the next phrase, outlining Jesus' response, unless you had a similar experience. Matthew writes, "Jesus did not answer a word." Such silence must have shaken her greatly.

This is a very interesting passage. The ONE who had compassion and healed many, now is silent to a need. The ONE who is the answer to any situation or circumstance is not answering. He is not saying, "yes," and fortunately, he is not yet saying "no," but He is saying nothing! The silence is deafening.

Ask anyone who is facing a dire need; such as praying for someone to come to Christ. Instead, of coming to Christ, the one they are praying for seem to run further away. It seems the heavens are silent.

Ask anyone who is praying for someone with illness. Instead of getting better, heaven is silent and they continue to worsen.

Ask those who are at the brink of financial ruin. They pray with great need. They know that their only hope is God. They pray, but again heaven is quiet and the future is bleak.

Not a sound, not a word is spoken.

Is this a "get God's attention" moment? Should we gain a new tactic of praying, if the method is wrong? The soul searching begins, and the silence continues.

It is the unspeakable of prayer: A silent heaven!

Discussing brass ceilings, or silent Majesty, is a low priority for most. Some would call these time's "faithless" times because of the silent outcome. They would say that the reason the heavens are silent due to one's miniscule faith. Therefore, they will try to build their faith. Others are like the disciples, and want to ignore the problem:

" So his disciples came to him and urged him, "Send her away, for she keeps crying out after us." Matt 15:23 (NIV)

Some do not want to be bothered. They say "send her away."

You pray for a need and such individuals are sitting on the sidelines like Job's friends. They are not intercessors for a need, they are the enemies of the needy. They spew rebuttals such as:

"Stop praying, you are bothering me!"

"It must not be God's will, since He is not answering!"

"Your problem is that you do not have enough faith."

The pat answers continue, but heaven remains silent.

What do you do when the heavens are silent?

To answer this question, one must look at the character of God. Many aspects of God's character are of great comfort to the prayer warrior, and a great beginning to getting an answer from God.

Although God may not be speaking, He <u>is</u> listening.

2

THE GOD WHO HEARS

There are some givens to our God. He has always revealed himself through his name, or revealed His character through His actions. God is very jealous of all of His characteristics. Those characteristics reveal Him to humanity and they are the realities of His existence. He is God and will have no other gods before Him. Not that God is afraid of any man-made god, but He is jealous for a relationship with humanity and desires everyone to call upon Him and to know Him.

God has always shown himself to be a God who hears. That distinguishes him from any other God. Man has manufactured gods for himself, but those gods cannot hear, let alone answer. When Elijah confronted the prophets of Baal in I Kings 18:24, he declared, "The God who answers is God." It would be very appropriate to say, "The God who HEARS and answers, is God.

Our God is very clear, "He is the God who hears." David writes in Psalms 65:2,

"O Lord who hears prayer, to you all men will come." (NIV)

This is an important distinction: Our God does hear! Even when we do not feel He hears, He does.

Look at the passage in Matthew 15:23 again:

"Jesus did not answer a word." (NIV)

Notice it does not say Jesus did not hear her. He simply said nothing. He had reason to remain silent, but the great underlying truth is that He heard.

You may not pray the most eloquent prayer, you may not have the best choice of words to articulate your need, and you may not have the "feeling" God is hearing you, but it is His nature to hear. He will hear His children when they call upon Him.

"He will call upon me, and I will answer him; I will be with him in trouble, I will deliver him and honor him. With long life will I satisfy him and show him my salvation." Ps 91:15-16 (NIV)

How can He answer lest He first hear the prayer? Is there a time He does not hear? According to Isaiah, our sin can keep our prayers from being heard. Not just answered, but even heard.

"Surely the arm of the LORD is not too short to save, nor his ear too dull to hear. But your iniquities have separated you from your God; your sins have hidden his face from you, *so that he will not hear.* " Isa 59:1-2 (NIV) (*emphasis mine*)

During times of prayer for a need, attention should be paid to the status of our walk with God. Is there sin unforgiven? Are there things between you and your God? Is it possible the reason the heavens are silent is because there is a hindrance due to sin keeping God from hearing your plea? Before going into great depth in prayer, one must do some soul searching.

Maybe there are problems between you and someone else.

Jesus said, "And when you stand praying, if you hold anything against anyone, forgive him, so that your Father in heaven may forgive you your sins." Mark 11:25 (NIV)

If the reason God has not answered your prayers is because of sin, sin will remain a barrier between you and answered prayer until you repent of that sin and ask Him for forgiveness.

Sin is always a barrier between mankind and God and could be the very thing standing in the way of your answered prayer.

For the child of God whose sins have been forgiven, the promise is true: He will hear you. Jeremiah says it in a greater way:

"For I know the plans I have for you," declares the LORD, "plans to prosper you and not to harm you, plans to give you hope and a future. *Then you will call upon me and come and pray to me, and I will listen to you.* You will seek me and find me when you seek me with all your heart." Jeremiah 29:11-13 (NIV) *(emphasis mine)*

The Canaanite woman's problem was not that her request was not heard, it was that there was no reply. Jesus did hear her. He hears us when we pray.

Who has prayed fervently to the Lord, with a very important need to be met, only to find the heavens silent to the requestor? I remember a time of praying while pastoring a church in Arkansas. During this particular time the ceilings seemed to be brass as I was pouring my soul out to God. Lest you think I lost my mind there, I felt a presence in the sanctuary and heard a whisper in my mind saying, "The Lord is not listening to you!" That statement, wherever it emanated from, energized my prayer life. I immediately turned and pointed into the air. "That is not what the Word of God says," I shouted to whatever or whoever initiated that whisper. I began to quote scriptures that indicated God's love for me, His desire for a relationship with me and His promise to hear me when I call upon Him.

There are very safe assumptions a prayer warrior can make. One is that God will forgive when we ask Him to forgive. Jesus came to redeem us from the curse of sin, to wash away our sin and to offer forgiveness and relationship with the Father. The other assumption is that when we are in right relationship with God, God will hear our prayer. Notice that I did not say God will always answer your prayer the way you want Him to. God is not at your disposal. He is not a genie in a bottle so that once we give the bottle a prayer rub, out pops a genie and we make our three wishes. If that is your idea of prayer, it is very probable that your prayer life is suffering greatly. God is not our servant; we are His. He is not our genie to grant us whatever selfish or even unselfish requests we make. Nevertheless, for those who call upon the Lord as His children, the safe assumption one can make is that we have an audience with the Lord of Glory. He does listen!

It should give us a great joy to know that our God delights in us as we call upon Him. We can come boldly before Him and present our requests to a God who listens.

"Let us then approach the throne of grace with confidence, so that we may receive mercy and find grace to help us in our time of need." Heb. 4:16 (NIV)

That should not give rise to a haughty attitude, nor should we feel that we can entreat Him in any way contrary to the honor and reverence He is due. But, we can come boldly before a hearing God.

God is jealous of His reputation as One who hears prayer. The writer of Hebrews takes this thought a little further:

"And without faith it is impossible to please God, because anyone who comes to him must believe that he exists and that he rewards those who earnestly seek him. Hebrews 11:6 (NIV)

There are two givens to this God-pleasing faith. *First,* those who seek to please God must believe in God. They must believe in Him, not an impersonal force, goodness or even the spirit of love, but they must believe in Him. *Second,* they must believe that God will reward those who seek Him. The unsaid part of this is that God is not far

The unsaid part of this is that God is not far removed from His people, and He delights when we draw near to Him.

removed from His people, and He delights when we draw near to Him. He desires a relationship with you and offers a hearing ear to listen to your heart. This kind of faith is the one that moves mountains and it is impossible to please God without it.

When the Canaanite woman came to Jesus, she made a safe assumption that Jesus would hear her. I am sure she understood, to some degree, that Jesus may not actually meet her need, but even that was a remote option for her. She came to Jesus so that Jesus would hear her and to have her need met.

Sometimes we are not thoroughly convinced that we are praying the express will of God, and may even question whether He is listening. Other times we may not pray as passionately as others and may feel that our praying is not as impressive to God's hearing as other more passionate praying people. This is a danger. Our prayers do need passion, but our walk with God should be gauge of passion rather than how loud or boisterous we are

> When we walk the godly walk, we can rest assured God hears the godly talk.

during prayer. When we walk the godly walk, we can rest assured God hears the godly talk. When we walk that godly walk, even a whisper of prayer echoes through the chambers of glory as God delights over us, hearing what we say.

3

No One Is Paying Attention

I am reminded of Elijah's comments as the prophets of Baal are calling upon their god.

"So they took the bull given them and prepared it. Then they called on the name of Baal from morning till noon. "O Baal, answer us!" they shouted. But there was no response; no one answered. And they danced around the altar they had made." I Kings 18:26-29 (NIV)

The picture of four hundred-fifty religious men jumping, praying and crying for their god to answer their prayers caused Elijah to taunt them:

"At noon Elijah began to taunt them. "Shout louder!" he said. "Surely he is a god! Perhaps he is deep in thought, or busy, or traveling. Maybe he is sleeping and must be awakened." So they shouted louder and slashed themselves with swords and spears, as was their custom, until their blood flowed. : I Kings 18:27 (NIV)

These men were very religious. They certainly did not lack zeal. If "prayer" was the answer, they prayed with passion. They tried. It was not their fault for trying. It was their fault for the choice of a god. Their god was not a god at all. He was merely a man made idol that could not speak, could not perform the needed miracle, and most importantly, <u>he could not hear</u>.

"Midday passed, and they continued their frantic prophesying until the time for the evening sacrifice. But there was no response, no one answered, no one paid attention." I Kings 18:29 (NIV)

No one paid attention! They had the passionate prayer, religious zeal and they had the altar ready to burn but no one was there to pay attention. *Their zeal meant nothing without the real.*

Now Elijah steps up to the altar to put His God to the test. He already put God on the line,

"The god who answers by fire-- he is God." (I Kings 18:24, NIV)

Of course, God had to hear first in order to answer. Elijah, armed with his audacious faith, steps up to the altar and asks them to douse the altar with water. Buckets and buckets of water. So much that the altar is saturated, the sacrifice is saturated and the water fills the trenches surrounding the altar. Some use water to put out a fire, but Elijah had so much faith he used fire to put out the water. What faith! Elijah had to know that His God was able to hear Him.

> Some use water to put out a fire, but Elijah had so much faith he used *fire* to put out the *water*. What faith!

"At the time of sacrifice, the prophet Elijah stepped forward and prayed: "O LORD, God of Abraham, Isaac and Israel, let it be known today that you are God in Israel and that I am your servant and have done all these things at your command. Answer me, O LORD, answer me, so these people will know that you, O LORD, are God, and that you are turning their hearts back again." Then the fire of the LORD fell and burned up the sacrifice, the wood, the stones and the soil, and also licked up the water in the trench." I Kings 18:36-38 (NIV)

The fire of the Lord fell because Elijah prayed. Elijah prayed because he knew his God was listening to his prayer and he was convinced his God could do more than he could ask or think.

> The fire of the Lord fell because Elijah prayed. Elijah prayed because he knew his God was listening to his prayer and he was convinced his God could do more than he could ask or think.

We have to have the same kind of faith. One that believes God hears and answers prayers. The mere fact that God was able to hear him gave him the courage to go beyond a mere burnt offering. His faith was audacious and it was audacious because Elijah knew God heard him pray.

We all have the capacity to pray Elijah-like prayers. However, not all achieve this kind of victory. Could it be because we are not always convinced that God hears us? David kept that in mind when he called on God in Psalms 17:

"I call on you, O God, for you will answer me; give ear to me and hear my prayer. Show the wonder of your great love, you who save by your right hand those who take refuge in you from their foes." Ps 17:6-7 (NIV)

The first thing to understand during those times when God says nothing is to KNOW that God hears you when you pray. That mindset and perception alone is enough to move God and should encourage you that even though He may not be speaking at that moment, He, the CREATOR of all things, our hope and life, God Himself, has heard you. He listens and hears. Start there and believe that because He hears and loves you, He will move on your behalf.

4

THE PLAYERS IN OUR PRAYERS

There are a number of players in our prayers. Some are encouraging and supportive. Others are the ones that hinder our spiritual progress. Still others fall somewhere in the middle. They mean well but do not always know the way God desires to move in our lives. The disciples were that kind of group.

Leave us alone!

"Jesus did not answer a word. So his disciples came to him and urged him, "Send her away, for she keeps crying out after us." Matthew 15:23 (NIV)

The disciples meant well in their attempt to shield Jesus from someone who would "bother" Him. They viewed the Canaanite woman as a distraction; one not worthy of making a sound within earshot of the Lord.

This was far from the truth. He did hear her despite the players in her prayers.

There are many players in our prayers. In this case, it was a group of followers of Christ. They were the ones that should have been the first to show compassion and faith, instead, they were tired of her requests. Sometimes even those who know the Lord miss divine appointments. These players did not have a clue as to what the possibilities were. They were not full of faith; they were full of frustration. "Send her away," they urged Christ, "she will not leave us alone." Their frustration could have served as an obstacle to this woman's request.

We can see the same type of players in prayers throughout the Word of God. Of course, they are always on the periphery. They are not major players unless one considers their words and heeds their complaints.

The prophets of Baal were players in Elijah's prayers. Daniel also had players in his prayers. Unfortunately, Daniels players sought to trap him by making it illegal to call upon the Lord in prayer.

While those players' desires were for selfish gain, one cannot underestimate the powerful influence that those players had in Daniels life.

"Now Daniel so distinguished himself among the administrators and the satraps by his exceptional qualities that the king planned to set him over the whole kingdom. At this, the administrators and the satraps tried to find grounds for charges against Daniel in his conduct of government affairs, but they were unable to do so. They could find no corruption in him, because he was trustworthy and neither corrupt nor negligent. Finally these men said, "We will never find any basis for charges against this man Daniel unless it has something to do with the law of his God." Daniel 6:3-5 (NIV)

The players to Daniels prayers continued:

"So the administrators and the satraps went as a group to the king and said: "O King Darius, live forever! The royal administrators, prefects, satraps, advisers and governors have all agreed that the king should issue an edict and enforce the decree that anyone who prays to any god or man during the next thirty days, except to you, O king, shall be thrown into the lions' den." Daniel 6:6-7 (NIV)

These players to Daniel's prayers attempted to make the very act of prayer illegal and the consequences fatal. They attempted to stop Daniel from the very act of prayer. Daniel could have allowed them to influence him from calling upon God. He could have allowed their extreme measures to hinder his faithful endeavors. We can allow those around us to hinder us from our faithful endeavors as well.

Players to our prayers can also intimidate you, or make you feel awkward for the very act of prayer: maybe at a restaurant over a meal, in a public setting, or before a group. You may feel intimidation to pray for guidance or to pray for needs in your life. You may feel that others will regard you as weak or shallow because of your simple prayers. If that is the case, then the players to your prayers have hindered you from receiving what you need from God.

Daniel was not going to allow the players in his life to squelch the prayers to His God.

"Now when Daniel learned that the decree had been published, he went home to his upstairs room where the windows opened toward Jerusalem. Three times a day he got down on his knees and prayed, giving thanks to his God, just as he had done before." Daniel 6:10 (NIV)

Daniel was not going to allow those self-seekers to keep Him from seeking God, regardless of the cost.

These players caught Daniel in the act of prayer. They brought him before the king who had approved the outlawing of prayer to God. The law stipulated capital punishment for the perpetrator of such a act. The sentence required that anyone caught praying be thrown into a lion's den. Unfortunately, for the king, the one caught was his trusted advisor Daniel. Now he had also become a player to Daniel's prayers. King Darius must have known that there was something different about Daniel when he said,

..."May your God, whom you serve continually, rescue you!" (Daniel 6:16, NIV)

And God did rescue Daniel. The lion's endured a long night of lock-jaw, the king endured a long night of sleeplessness and Daniel slept with large purring felines. The players in Daniel's prayers could not deter him from the great outcome he won, nor could they speak into the different needs Daniel faced.

Sometimes well-meaning people are players in your prayers, sometimes you will contend with self-seeking people and sometimes you will find the players in your prayers are malicious in their attempts to keep you from seeking God. But seek God you must. Whether He answers immediately or not, the actual act of praying cannot be deterred from the task at hand. The players to Daniel's prayers won a temporary victory, but not the eternal war. It may seem that those around you are willing to use coercion or intimidation to keep you from praying, but you must not let them succeed.

> Sometimes well-meaning people sometimes are the players to your prayers, sometimes you will contend with self-seeking people and sometimes you will find the players in your prayers are malicious in their attempts to keep you from seeking God. But seek God you must!

Daniels dedication to prayer won the victory for him, despite the activities of these players. We cannot ever shrink from seeking God either. We cannot allow the players around us to determine what happens in us, especially when we have great needs to take before God in prayer. God alone should determine the outcome of the prayer, not be kept from hearing the prayer altogether.

For the Canaanite woman, it would have been easy to allow those around her to determine her future. She could have been hurt and could have walked away in emotional pain. There is something to be said for desperation, however. She was a woman on a mission. Her goal was for the Lord to hear her and she would not allow anything or anyone to determine whether she found success. Lack of passion would have kept her from further pursuing Christ.

It is not always people that play a part in our prayers. Sometimes it is passivity. The spirit of passivity can keep you from taking the matter before God in the desperate tone needed. Jesus spoke to laying hold of kingdom things in a forceful way in Matthew:

"From the days of John the Baptist until now, the kingdom of heaven has been forcefully advancing, and forceful men lay hold of it." Matthew 11:12 (NIV)

If your child is sick, and you love your child, you will seek the very best for your child. If a doctor has shown success in treating the malady diagnosed in your child, then you would do everything in your power to see that doctor. If it were life and death, you would demonstrate passion by your desperation. Nothing would stand in your way.

Our passionate seeking after God cannot be weak or transitory. If it is, then the players in our prayers can hinder us from getting the help we need.

Sometimes, however, the players in our prayers can help us find the answer we seek. Jesus had traveled to a secluded place away from people to rest. Upon returning, He came to a house where a large group of people began to congregate to hear and see Him. So many came, those who could not squeeze into the house crowded outside near windows and doors.

Several men, who had heard Jesus was near, went to a paralyzed friend and carried him to Jesus.

"Since they could not get him to Jesus because of the crowd, they made an opening in the roof above Jesus and, after digging through it, lowered the mat the paralyzed man was lying on. When Jesus saw their faith, he said to the paralytic, "Son, your sins are forgiven." Mark 2:4-5 (NIV)

While we do not know whose idea it was to get the paralytic to Christ, their determination was exceptional. Several facts stand out in this passage:

First, the players to the paralyzed man's prayers were not going to allow people to get in the way of getting their friend healing. Just as in Daniel's case, people can be an obstacle that stand between you and God. Your goal and passion must be to get past people so that they do not determine whether you can touch God or not. While some may have come to see Jesus out of curiosity, or the desire to see a famous person, these men were there because they had a friend who had serious need, and Jesus could meet the need.

Second, they had to bypass walls and structures that presented a barrier between them and God. For you,

those walls may not be stone or mud, but may be
unforgiveness or sin. It may be pride or jealousy. The
player to your prayer may be past hurts that continue
to play a part in your present circumstances.
Anything that stands between you and your miracle
must go! All principalities and powers, all structures,
whether built by you or others must never keep you
from what you need from God.

Third, for the men carrying the paralytic, they also
had to overcome a final barrier. It was the barrier
standing between them and Christ: the roof. The Bible
says they dug through the roof. They
were determined that nothing would
separate them from an answer. For
them, Christ rewarded their faith
once their friend was lowered
through the roof. The roof was the lid that could
potentially keep them from their miracle, but even that
lid was not strong enough to keep them from what
they wanted for their friend. The limit to your God-
given potential is always going to a part of your life,
unless you break through the lid. It will be the barrier
that stands between you and the miracle. In order to

> What lid is keeping you from Jesus?

see your miracle, you must go beyond the lid that keeps you from Christ! What lid is keeping you from Jesus?

That lid may be the very thing keeping you from an answer, so you must dig deep to get past it.

Imagine for a moment being that paralytic as your friends are lowering you through the roof, down into a crowded room, right in front of Jesus. The determination on their faces, the set jaws, the eyes of anticipation and muscles tightening as they lower you would create joy in your heart. You would be so thankful for these players in your prayers. What friends they are, you would think! Nothing has kept them from seeking the miracle you so desperately needed. You can picture your four friends peering through an opening in the roof so full of joy and anticipation for you as they lower you down. You can see their smiles, their thumbs up, high fives to each other for accomplishing all they could. They had become players in your prayer in a powerful and positive way, but now it was time for them to get out of the way too. The only thing between you and Christ is air, with all barriers removed.

Everything that occurred, as your friends were players in your prayers, has now made the difference in your life in the most profound way.

Here is what the Bible records when the friends had ended their service for the paralytic, and the words that meant complete and total healing for the paralytic:

When Jesus saw their faith, he said to the paralytic, "Son, your sins are forgiven." Mark 2:5 (NIV)

As this paralytic learned, faith is the key that opens heaven's doors. It was the determined faith of the friends, the expectant faith of the paralytic and the sovereign work of Christ that produced the miracle.

It began with the players. It can end with the players. We can live with our malady by allowing the players in our prayers to keep us from the victory we so desperately need. We can also see miracles when the players to our prayers stand *with us* in our distress, place us in front of Christ, and prepare us for the miracle we seek. In the final analysis, when the dust finally settles, though, we must not allow anything or anyone come between us and the God we seek.

The Canaanite woman had to get past the players, even ignoring them to speak to the answer to her problem. In the end, the only players in our prayers must be you and God. Once that is settled, then divine dialogue begins.

5

WHEN GOD SPEAKS

After distractions, and the players to your prayers
have been dealt with, then somewhere in the process
you can expect to hear from God.

That's exactly what happened in our text. It goes on to
say:

"Then Jesus said to the woman, "I was sent only to help
God's lost sheep—the people of Israel."" Matthew 15:24
(NLT)

Hearing from God may arrive in the form of
various means:

First, hearing from God may come from reading
God's Word (the Bible). You will find that suddenly
you come to the place where God's Word becomes
three-dimensional; where God's words literally leap
off the page directly into your spirit. Some call this a
quickening of God's Spirit or a *rhema* Word. It is that

moment where God speaks something through His Word directly into your life and you understand it powerfully, and immediately, that God has spoken to you through His Word.

This is a tricky area. Sometimes we read something into the passage that is not there, nor is it meant to be there. You must make sure you are reading right and not wanting something so bad that everything is saying what you want it to say. Context is key, and the first level of Bible reading. Read the context first, then understand who and what issue is being addressed. Finally, allow the Holy Spirit to speak to you from your reading of the Bible.

We must ensure that we are not reading something into scripture that the scripture is not saying. The same goes for sermons we hear.

I had that happen not too long ago. I was talking to a friend of mine who is getting an advanced degree. He was telling me that he had heard one of my messages and received an answer to prayer out of it. I was confused as I was not sharing anything about God's will, nor did I remember directly speaking something that could be construed as a word from God for anyone. He shared the "word" he heard me speak. I did not say what he thought I said. No problem, the Holy Spirit sometimes does that.

My friend, Greg Hackett, calls these times "Holy Spirit rabbit trails" that the Holy Spirit takes us on. Greg shared that we think a lot faster than people speak. Sometimes when someone is sharing God's Word, we think that person is saying something specific, but they did not share specific to your situation. The Holy Spirit can speak during that time and give us revelation to God's will.

Did my friend have that kind of experience, or was he wanting the answer so desperately to be "yes", that was what he "heard"? So, I questioned him further. I asked him if he was really hearing from God or if he wanted it so badly that he "heard" what he wanted to hear.

We can regard this better by using the term "revelation". Usually a revelation comes that quickens our heart to the answer from God's Word. We usually know if something we read in His Word speaks directly to our situation. Rightly interpreting God's Word is imperative to our seeking His face and hearing Him speak through scripture. So is "hearing" God speak to our spirit.

After extensively questioning my friend, I felt and he confirmed that God had indeed spoken to him and his life situation has borne that out. Praise God!

God does not always speak to us in the "yes" and he does not always speak in the "no" through His Word. The important thing to do when He speaks is to listen and do!

> "Warning, Will Robinson, Warning"...from Lost In Space

The *second* way God speaks to us is through other people. I hear the famous words from "Lost In Space" playing in my head now: "WARNING, WILL ROBINSON, WARNING!" Warning is the key here. If done correctly, words from others can confirm what God is speaking to you, or can help you to understand God's plan once He confirms it later. I have had people with a "word from God" for me that was NOT a word from God at all, and if I had heeded that word, I would have been disobedient to the true will of God. Be very careful listening to someone else who has heard from God on your behalf.

There is a powerful example of this in First Kings 13. God had spoken to a prophet of God to go and prophecy against King Jeroboam. God gave the young prophet a direct word: "You must not eat or drink anything while you are there, and should not return to Judah by the same way you came." After successfully prophesying, this young prophet left King Jeroboam and began his return home. Shortly thereafter, this young prophet encountered an "old prophet" who convinced the young prophet to disregard the word of the Lord. He even said, "I too am a prophet of the Lord...you can listen to me". Because of this blatant disregard for the "direct command" of God, this young prophet of God came under judgment from the Lord. God judged the young prophet for his disobedience and allowed a lion to kill him.

The tragedy of this story is that the young prophet trusted someone who had contradicted the very word of God, causing him to sin. I have always wondered why the "old prophet" tempted the "young prophet" to sin, and sometimes I get angry with the "old prophet" who should have known better. He encouraged disobedience and the "young prophet" listened. Ultimately, however, the young prophet had a responsibility to God. He failed in obedience and it cost him his life.

We must heed the warning the passage passively provides. There are times God's Word (the Bible) directly commands something, but someone we greatly respect or trust encourages us to disobey God's Word. Regardless of the status of the "prophet", and despite their understanding of the way God moves and works, we cannot give into the temptation to disobey a directive given in God's Word.

Do not dismiss a "word from the Lord" from other people immediately, unless it runs contrary to scripture. Then, regardless of who said it, refuse it. If it does line up, or is not in contradiction with God's Word, do not accept it until there is confirmation first, or at some point. Otherwise, someone's *agenda* may become your downfall. They may "call you" to China, but it may be because they want your position and "prophecy" out of agenda instead of out of the work of the Holy Spirit. We can be so hungry for God to speak, that we will listen to almost anything, hoping that it will be good for us. The scripture is clear what to do when people want to tell you what God is saying:

"Let two or three people prophesy, and let the others evaluate what is said." 1 Corinthians 14:29

The Spirit and the Word **always** agree

Do not accept anything said to you without evaluating what is being said. *First* against scripture; the Spirit and the Word **always** agree.

Second, evaluate it against what God has already spoken to you. If it confirms something God has already said to you, then you are in a good place to know God's heart better. If it does not confirm something God is already speaking to you, then wait, and do not accept it until God confirms that word in other ways. Why? Scripture bears out that you are a priest unto God and are responsible to hear from God yourself. You are responsible to approach God yourself.

You are responsible for your life and the way you live your life. You will one day give an account for your life. Hearing, and obeying the heart of God is crucial for that day you stand before Him.

It is important to remember that when you stand before God on that day, you will answer for all of your decisions, even if you followed the advice of a trusted friend. God bases rewards on your completion of His will for your life, not based on whether someone gave you a word from God. You must be loyal to God first, and then weigh what people say against God's Word, God's leading, and the activity of God in your life.

God also speaks to you, directly and into your spirit. Once, my mother shared that she had been praying for a long time about a problem and her prayers were not being answered at all, and it seemed they were not even reaching the ears of God. The problem was not getting better. Early one morning, about 4 a.m., she was awake but still in bed, crying out to God about the problem. As she prayed, something happened. She explained it by saying, "John, God spoke to me and told me that it was all going to be alright." I asked, "How did you know it was God speaking to you?" She replied, "It was like thunder in my soul and I knew it was him."

Jesus said, "My sheep know my voice and a stranger they will not follow" John 10:27 (NLT)

It is important for you to hear from God from time to time. If you have not, make sure you are listening. Make sure there is no sin in your life. Make sure you are right with God and that you are living your life in a God-pleasing way.

When God says nothing, and then suddenly begins speaking, there may be more going on than you know.

6

JESUS CARES, HE'S JUST NOT CONCERNED

Reading our text, it would seem that Jesus was not interested in the Canaanite woman's need at all. I would say that most of the time we are more concerned about our need than we should be...and we interpret His response to our needs as unconcerned altogether.

Think about it for a moment, though. You may say, Jesus was not as concerned about her need as he should have been. We say that about the one who MADE everything out of nothing.

Frank Turet, speaking on Focus On The Family's "BIG DIG" DVD Series asked, "What was the greatest miracle ever recorded ?" Answering his own question, he said, "Yes, some say the resurrection but I believe that the greatest miracle was not the resurrection but creation." He continued that if God could step out on nothing, speak life into utter darkness, and create everything in our known world, resurrection is no problem. I agree!

Think about it this way. If you came to me and said, "John, I have a huge need. I am behind on my house payment by $200,000 and if I do not pay the entire $200,000 by this Wednesday, they will come and force me out of my house. If I do not pay it by Wednesday, I will be homeless."

I will feel bad for you, but I would know that I do not have that kind of money. I would be helpless and worried for you. I would feel for you but would be personally unable to give you or provide you with $200,000.

But, if I had one billion dollars in the bank, and you came to me and said, "John, I don't know what I am going to do. The electric company is going to shut off my electricity if I don't pay my bill by Wednesday. The bill is $150 and I simply don't have the money."

If I cared about you and loved you, I would not be concerned about it...not because I don't care, but because to meet that need would be nothing for me. I make enough in interest on my billion dollars *to buy the electric company.* So, you may search for a worried expression on my face, but you will not see it because it is not a worry... I have more than enough to cover the need.

If I am going to come to God and look for a concerned expression on God's countenance because of my need, it will never, ever happen. He will not wring his hands, or pace the floors worried over the situation. He will not be concerned to the point of fretting or being disturbed.

If you are trying to get God to notice your need, and have not had any success, then maybe you need to focus on something other than the problem.

> If you are trying to get God to notice your need, and have not had any success, then maybe you need to focus on something other than the problem.

God will never appear worried or

concerned about the problem.

Does that mean he does not care? Certainly not! He cares. Is He concerned? Not at all! It has nothing to do with whether He cares or not, but it has everything to do with His ability. If you are looking for God to be your worrywart, forget it. If you want Him to RSVP your pity party, it is not going to happen. If you want God to pace the floor worried how you are going to make it, look for another god that is unable to meet the need.

If, however, you want Him to meet your need, you've come to the right God. God is not worried about your need because He has the power to meet it. If He is not worried about it, then your worry will not move him to action.

Your fretting over it will not cause Him to move faster.

Your fretting will not move Him to action because He made everything and has all power. He does not have to prove anything to anyone.

So if worry, fear, fretting, or concern will not move God to action, what does?

7

SOME STORMS ARE BLESSINGS!

Look at the dialogue a little further.

When the Canaanite woman approached Jesus, there was no concern shown at all, but after He finally spoke, notice the response from the woman:

"But she came and worshiped him, pleading again, "Lord, help me!" Matthew 15:25 (NLT)

The sweet sound of His voice was music to her ears. She responded to His words with worship! Now you should hear the beeping sound of a bus backing up.

She heard Him right. She responded just like anyone who is focused rightly should respond; worshipping Him!

"Jesus responded, "It isn't right to take food from the children and throw it to the dogs." Matthew 15:26 (NLT)

From the outside, looking in, this is a very cutting statement. Christ was talking about the way the Jews viewed Gentile women. Jews had such a disdain for Gentiles, they considered them nothing more than a dog—and not a purebred one at that.

Again, before you look at this through your culture, or your thinking, remember this was not a description of His thoughts about the world. It was a view of culture of the day, and I believe He said it to gain a response from this Gentile woman.

Sometimes our perspective of the problem is wrong. Not every storm is from the enemy and not every blessing is from the Lord. God may not have given you the job to bless the kingdom of God; instead, it may be a trap from the enemy of your soul to keep you from doing God's will.

Satan may not have sent the storm you are in. God may have allowed it to bring you into a greater appreciation of His grace, His mercy, or His power. Your response is the key. You may have thought it was God or Satan because you reasoned it out.

Regardless of its origin, the response you have to the storm or the blessing is the key.

In his book, *Spurgeon on Prayer and Spiritual Warfare,* Charles Spurgeon writes, "I write this with all reverence: God Himself cannot deliver a person who is not in trouble. Therefore, it is to some advantage to be in distress, because God can then deliver you. Even Jesus Christ, the Healer of me, cannot heal a person who is not sick. Therefore, sickness is not an adversity for us, but rather an advantageous opportunity for Christ to heal us. The point is, my reader, your adversity may prove your advantage by offering occasion for the display of divine grace."

> God Himself cannot deliver a person who is not in trouble. Therefore, it is to some advantage to be in distress, because God can then deliver you.~ Charles Spurgeon

It is a test!

I believe we are tested continually. When we are tested, our response is always the key. The response will determine whether we have victory or not. It is not the wound that hurts us; it is our response to it.

For example, you cannot dictate how people treat you, or what they say about you, or even if they hurt you. You cannot dictate someone's actions at all. They may say good things, or they may say bad things about you. They may bless you or curse you. The key is not what they do. We have no control over that. The response to what they do matters the most.

That is the key in the response of the Gentile woman, and the key in your life. If you are going to live the kind of life God designed for you to live, you will have to understand that you will not be loved by all; never go through hard times, or that you are somehow immune to trouble.

Bad things will happen to you. To believe you are immune to problems is neither realistic nor biblical.

You will have trouble. That is a guarantee no matter how godly you are. You will go through trials, sometimes often.

The key is for you to overcome such situations by your response.

That is why Jesus gave us many thoughts about how we should respond to others.

Love those that hate you

Pray for those who use you

Forgive those who hurt you

Care for those who do not care for you

Are you responding to the problems in your life with faith, or with complaining?

Are you believing God, or focusing on what others are saying and doing? Are you reacting with anger and hurt, or responding with joy and an expectation of God's help?

You are tested by your reaction much more than by what happens to you. Your reaction is the only thing you control.

If you only focus on the things that have hurt you, it internalizes the pain, which will be detrimental to your faith and answered prayer. Over time, you will become discouraged.

If you continue to watch people, you will quickly surmise that people are not perfect, even those you look up to will fail your "perfection test" after a time. If you focus on people long enough, and the hurt they have caused, you will begin to internalize what you see, and you will become disillusioned.

But if you look to Christ, look fully to Him, you will be delivered. He is the answer you are seeking, He is the joy that you have always longed for, the peace that you so desperately crave.

What do you keep looking around for? What do you keep looking down about? Look at the face of Jesus. When you see His face, nothing else matters. If you do that, and internalize that, God will deliver you!

Your response to life is what opens the door to your miracle. It is not your need that drives God to meet your need, but it is your response to your need that will make the difference.

Here are some very important questions to ask yourself regarding your need:

How are you responding to your pressure?

How are you responding to your situation?

How are you responding to your hurt?

If you respond the right way, you will open the door to your miracle.

Are you having a hard time responding the right way? Are you struggling with knowing how to respond?

If so, that may be the greatest need you have, not the one that occupies all your prayer time.

Once divine dialogue begins, your response will determine your success, not what was said by others.

8

BEWARE OF THE COMPARISON TRAP

There is a subtle trap that finds its way into our prayer life, and into the way we expect God to move in our lives.

Again, we read,

"Jesus responded, "It isn't right to take food from the children and throw it to the dogs." Matthew 15:26 (NLT)

This part of the prayer time is crucial. This woman was an outsider...not a daughter of Abraham. She was not "chosen", nor was she favored by any stretch of the imagination. She had no rights to kingdom privileges.

She could have compared her need to the children of Israel's provision.

Jesus called out the distinction between the chosen people of God (the Jews) and the rest of the world who were considered dogs. The distinction He made could have caused her to get into the comparison trap.

You have to be very careful that you do not fall into the comparison trap. If you do, you will miss out on the answered prayer you are so desperately seeking.

> What does that comparison trap look like? It is when you compare your problem to other people's provision.

What does that comparison trap look like? It is when you compare your problem to other people's provision.

In other words, you may be sick and see someone well and compare your need to their provision by praying, "Lord, why are other people well, and I am going through such a trial in my body?"

Or you may see an unbeliever without a financial care in the world, and you love God and wonder why you are not blessed financially. You may compare your need to their provision. You may ask the Lord, "Lord, why are they well off, and I barely make it on my income."

Be careful and **DO NOT COMPARE YOUR PROBLEM TO OTHER PEOPLE'S PROVISION**. That possibility is always a temptation to anyone needing a miracle from God. It can come close to coveting.

For the Gentile woman, she could have found herself comparing her need to other people's provision:

They were chosen, she was a Gentile.

They were the king's kids, she was considered a dog.

They were who Jesus came for, she was an unnecessary distraction.

You can be tempted to fall into the comparison trap too, especially when you struggle, pray, fast, believe and watch as someone who does not seem to break a sweat seems to get ahead. They have quick victory. They leave you in their dust and you are left wondering how the "chosen" are chosen and why you are not at the same level they are. It is the comparison trap and you must do everything to keep yourself from falling into that trap.

The worst part of the comparison trap is that it breeds questions in you that will cause you to feel your need very acutely, and you will notice everyone's blessing. You will question God's love, care, and desire to help you in your situation. Such feelings run contrary to faith.

Worse yet, the comparison trap sounds very much like coveting. Coveting someone's provision is dangerous. It will endanger your answer from God.

There are subtle cues to every part of our prayer time. There are responses that speak into our prayer time. Players to our prayers can speak into our prayer time, or the depth of our need may speak into our prayer time. Our hope that God will take pity on us and move in our situation because we are comparing someone's provision to our need may also speak into our prayer time. But, eventually, our response will dictate whether we will have an answer or not! It is the right response that will make the difference, all the difference, in seeing God move on your behalf.

I can hear you say,..."Ok, what then, is the right response?"

9

THE RIGHT RESPONSE

We should look at this Canaanite woman, who responded the right way. She responded based on the character of God.

She seized on an opportunity of God's character that you can seize as well.

THE BIG WORD FOR FAITH: ULTRAFIDIAN FAITH

"Jesus responded, "It isn't right to take food from the children and throw it to the dogs." She replied, "That's true, Lord, but even dogs are allowed to eat the scraps that fall beneath their masters' table." Matthew 15:26-27 (NLT)

What is the opportunity she seized? It was to call on who Jesus was, and what He could do. She responded through a trusting faith.

How do I know that? Because she talked about the crumbs that fell from the master's table.

Think about her response for a moment. She could have said, "All I want is the miracle"...or "I want the scraps from the table" indicating that she wanted to get what the kids did not want. Leftovers! It would be like the broccoli on my plate (I would gladly give it to the dogs).

Instead, she indicated an even smaller portion was all she needed. She did not want what they did not want, she just wanted a crumb that fell from the bread. It was so small, and insignificant that the children would not even give a second thought about brushing it off the table and sweeping it up. She, however, indicated that all she wanted was a crumb (in the Greek, the word is *"psichion"* meaning small particle or bit). All she needed was a crumb, because a crumb from the masters table, while insignificant for the children, was more than enough to provide all she needed.

If it is nothing for God to raise the dead, and create the universe, then the greatest need you could have is nothing that cannot be met by an insignificant crumb from His table.

To know this truth in your mind is important, but to call that out in prayer in relation to your need is crucial. To call that out is to call out the very nature of who Jesus was and is. This Gentile woman called out the creative nature of Christ.

That is exactly what the book of John calls out.

In the beginning was the Word, the Word was with God and the Word was God, the same was in the beginning with God. All things were made by Him and without Him was not anything made that was made." John 1:1-2 (NLT)

So, this Gentile woman inferred that she only needed the crumbs left over, the one's that fall from the master's table, to meet her need. The small, the insignificant, microscopic crumbs were enough.

That is a powerful thought. Just a crumb. Just a little bit...just one word from God...just one thing from Him and that is enough.

That is the key to her response and to this story. It is the key to her answered prayer. It was a God opportunity that she seized, one that spoke into her situation, and caused Jesus to take note.

You will not get the Lord's attention by calling attention to your need. He already knows your need. Nor is He impressed with the size of your need. Jesus did not call attention to the needs of any New Testament story.

Never in God's Word did Jesus say, "Wow, You've got a great need". "Your need is bigger than anyone else's need". He never told anyone, "Whoa, dude, you've got a big problem."

He never called attention to the need, and when individuals did, He did not spend time contemplating the depth of the need. He did not recite the kind of statement some in the mental health field would recite, "It sounds like you have a great need, one that is keeping you up at night, how do you feel about that?"

Instead, Jesus always looked for those who understood faith, or expressed it.

I mentioned the four men who carried their friend to Jesus earlier. The Bible never said, "when Jesus saw the depth of the need, he made the paralyzed walk". He did not say, "Oh, I'm sorry you can't walk"…"or dude, you can't walk." Instead, in Mark 2:5, the Bible says,

"When Jesus *saw their faith*, he said to the paralytic, "Son, your sins are forgiven." (emphasis mine) (NLT)

Then he healed the paralytic.

In, Mark 4:40, Jesus had just commanded the winds and waves to be quiet, and be still, and they obeyed. The disciples could not believe what they had just experienced, and Jesus could not believe that they were still struggling with faith after witnessing so many miracles. Then he turned to the disciples and said, "Why are you so afraid? Do you still have no faith?"

The woman with the issue of blood touched the hem of Jesus garment, and immediately Jesus knew someone had touched him. When he turned around and asked, "Who touched my clothes?" the disciples could not believe he was asking such a question. Everyone was trying to touch Jesus. He was in a huge crowd of people and everyone wanted to touch Him. However, that was not what He meant. He was not talking about who was closest to Him, or who brushed against his body. He was talking about the one that touched Him with faith. This faith was the one thing that caused Him to stop in His tracks; It was one the thing that caused Him to wonder who dared to touch Him; It was one the thing that changed the woman's life.

This faith is the ONE thing that the Bible says will please God! Your faith in Him is the one thing that will cause God to stop and pay attention to you. However, that is not the faith most know.

10

What Kind of Faith Is This

You have probably come this far in the book and know most of what has been shared. You may even feel like you have done it all, with little response from God. Nevertheless, there is a common component that has yet to be addressed, and one that every person in the Bible who received a miracle found to be necessary.

The kind of faith demonstrated in the story in Matthew 15 is not a static, passive faith. It is not an ignorant-of-the-circumstances belief. In fact, this faith compares the problem to Christ and finds it insufficient to warrant fear. It is a faith that has confidence, trust, daring, and boldness fully placed in God. It is an audacious, over-the-top faith.

It is not the faith of antiquity or the faith of a dead generation. This kind of faith is a very active creature, full of life, daring and bold. This faith has nerve, gall and determination. It is not simple, nor is it passive. It is profound and unwavering. It believes despite the circumstances, hopes despite the odds and steps out on air to find firmness to stand on.

It laughs at calamity, balks at uncertainty, and looks at the storm as an opportunity for God to do the incredible.

It is the kind of faith that does not merely *slap fear* in the face, it is the kind of faith that literally turns on fear and rends it to pieces. It is a faith that causes every demon in hell to fear, and every saint to rejoice. It is the one thing, and the only thing that causes God pleasure. Ultrafidian faith is the faith that finds the smallest, weakest, most inept person and calls them to greatness, strength, and ability to move mountains.

When the lion roars against this ultrafidian kind of faith, ultrafidian faith takes a baseball bat and goes lion hunting. Every spiritual lion attacking this faith must be wary. This kind of faith will not run. Every tormenting fear must look-out, as this kind of faith will sniff out every fear and rip it to shreds.

So what is ultrafidian faith? It is the faith that goes beyond mere faith. It is not what most possess and even fewer demonstrate.

Intimidation hides from this ultrafidian kind of faith.

That is why Jesus said to the woman, "your faith is great." It was ultrafidian faith and it was THE faith that moved Christ to action.

It is THE thing that will move Him to action on your behalf as well.

It is something that every miracle Jesus performed has in common. Regardless of the situation, regardless of the miracle needed, each miracle required this ultrafidian faith.

The common definition for the word "ultrafidian" is simply: "beyond faith."

This may be a new word, but the idea has been around for thousands of years.

My definition of "ultrafidian faith" is a loud, audacious, confident, full of belief, over-the-top, beyond the common every day faith. Ultrafidian faith screams out trust, obedience, and belief in God when prevailing circumstances would usually take us another direction.

It has little to do with your salvation so much as it has to do with your attitude, your mindset, and your walk with God. Ultrafidian faith is a faith that will step out, step up, pray down, pull down, praise God and build up in response to the obedience God calls us to express.

It expresses loudly, with great confidence in God, and will back up that faith with counterintuitive actions. It seems that when people do this, God is well-pleased and miracles happen.
Every...single...time!

It's not just "faith" as most people see faith. It is not simply "trust" as most people see trust. It is not merely "belief." The person that has "ultrafidian faith" has moved beyond the realm of merely believing in God, into an arena of expectation and trust that overwhelms the problem and brings about a

God-given solution. Their actions prove that "ultrafidian faith" delights our Creator.

Look at the miracles in both the Old Testament, and the New Testament and see the "ultrafidian faith" demonstrated.

In I Kings 18, Elijah was confronted with the prophets of Baal. He demanded they prove whose God was real, and the real God of Israel. In the confrontation, Elijah tells them to call upon their god, then Elijah would call on His God and the God that answered by fire would be God. He certainly had faith, and that was a faith move as represented as his audacity.

So, the prophets of Baal kill a sacrificial bull, lay it in pieces on the altar and call on their god all day long. They dance, they cut themselves, and all the while, Elijah taunts them. That was a faith move on Elijah's part. He knew his God was real, and their god was a sham.

After they prayed, cried, and tried with all their might to have their god answer, they finally gave up their plight. So, Elijah rebuilt the altar in the name of the Lord(a key in this exchange), and dug a trench around the altar deep enough to hold about four gallons of water.

Then, Elijah started demonstrating ultrafidian faith. He ordered those helping him to fill large jars with water and pour it on the offering and the wood. He did this again, and then, ordered it done a third time.

Water soaked the wood, the slain bull parts, and then ran down into the trench and filled it as well. In total, there was probably around 20-25 gallons of water poured on the altar.

With each pouring, with each step in this process, Elijah expressed ultrafidian faith to God. He did not express faith with mere words, but with his actions. It was audacious faith. It was confident faith. It was "ultrafidian faith."

Then, the scene unfolds with a simple prayer:

"At the usual time for offering the evening sacrifice, Elijah the prophet walked up to the altar and prayed, "O LORD, God of Abraham, Isaac, and Jacob, prove today that you are God in Israel and that I am your servant. Prove that I have done all this at your command. O LORD, answer me! Answer me so these people will know that you, O LORD, are God and that you have brought them back to yourself." Immediately the fire of the LORD flashed down from heaven and burned up the young bull, the wood, the stones, and the dust. It even licked up all the water in the trench! 1 Kings 18:36-38 (NLT)

Again, most would pour some type of flammable liquid to start a fire...so that just a spark will do. Instead, Elijah does the counterintuitive, ultrafidian faith sort of thing...by pouring water.

Some people put water to stop a fire, but this "ultrafidian faith" was the very element that put Elijah over the top in the faith column, and screamed, "I believe" in ways that mere words could never imitate.

Then, the Bible records the response of the people: "And when all the people saw it, they fell face down on the ground and cried out, "The LORD—he is God! Yes, the LORD is God!" 1 Kings 18:39 (NLT)

After seeing the incredible, of course people would express that God is God. They will express trust and faith when they see Him do the incredible, but it was the "ultrafidian faith" of Elijah that caused this event to end in total victory.

It is that ultrafidian faith throughout scripture that brought so many to the beginning of miracles.

Look at most every miracle, from the widow woman at Zarephath (1 Kings 17:7-23), where Elijah requested that she use the very last portion of their provisions to feed the prophet, to the miraculous raising of her son from the dead. His "ultrafidian faith" and her powerful obedience brought about an oil vessel and flour canister that never emptied until the drought was over.

The story of Joshua and the children of Israel's victory at Jericho also demonstrates "ultrafidian faith". The book of Joshua records the instructions God gave Joshua:

"But the LORD said to Joshua, "I have given you Jericho, its king, and all its strong warriors. You and your fighting men should march around the town once a day for six days. Seven priests will walk ahead of the Ark, each carrying a ram's horn. On the seventh day you are to march around the town seven times, with the priests blowing the horns. When you hear the priests give one long blast on the rams' horns, have all the people shout as loud as they can. Then the walls of the town will collapse, and the people can charge straight into the town." Joshua 6:1-5 (NLT)

The faith God called Joshua to express was "ultrafidian faith." They were to march around a fortified city and express complete and total trust in God. They were to walk in obedience without brandishing spears, or producing a nuclear weapon. Then, on the final day, the priests were to blow horns as they marched around the walls seven times.

Then, a shout went up. After the shout went up, the walls came down. They expressed "ultrafidian faith" then shouted at the conclusion for "For the Lord has given you the city!" It was promised, and they claimed what God had promised.

They won that victory because of their ultrafidian faith, not because of military enablement, nor the extraordinary skills of the trumpeters, nor the precision marching of the people. It was the "ultrafidian faith" they exhibited that caused the walls to come down.

That is where trust gets its greatest power. When we trust God beyond what makes sense and obey Him in what seems ridiculous, when He calls for it, that trust becomes a catalyst to our victory.

If one could ask King Jehoshaphat if he felt foolish when he was surround by the Moabites, Ammonites, and some of the Meunites armies, he would have probably said, "yes," if he had considered the actions. Those enemies of Judah had declared war on Jehoshaphat and the Bible declares that Jehoshaphat had proclaimed a fast and sought the help of the Lord. That was faith. He expressed belief, but not ultrafidian faith.

The Bible declares in 2 Chronicles 20:14 that the Spirit of the Lord came upon Jahaziel son of Zechariah. He shared the word of the Lord and that word said, "The battle is not yours, but God's...then went on to say...

"Tomorrow, march out against them. You will find them coming up through the ascent of Ziz at the end of the valley that opens into the wilderness of Jeruel. But you will not even need to fight. Take your positions; then stand still and watch the LORD's victory. He is with you, O people of Judah and Jerusalem. Do not be afraid or discouraged. Go out against them tomorrow, for the LORD is with you!" 2 Chronicles 20:16-17 (NLT)

The people heard this word and expressed audible praise to God with a 'very loud voice'. They expressed faith, but then Jehoshaphat did the counterintuitive. He expressed "ultrafidian faith" the next morning when they were to begin their march against the enemy.

"On the way Jehoshaphat stopped and said, "Listen to me, all you people of Judah and Jerusalem! Believe in the LORD your God, and you will be able to stand firm. Believe in his prophets, and you will succeed." After consulting the people, the king appointed singers to walk ahead of the army, singing to the LORD and praising him for his holy splendor. This is what they sang: "Give thanks to the LORD; his faithful love endures forever!" 2 Chronicles 20:20-21 (NLT)

Think about this for a minute. If you are going to fight a skilled adversary, you want your skilled warriors in front of the army. You do not want your inexperienced people there, and certainly do not want the church choir out front (unless you have had enough with the church choir).

But, in a counterintuitive move, an "ultrafidian faith" move…Jehoshaphat sends the choir out front. Their job was to praise God. Not to fight, or even engage the enemy; they were not to take up one sword or spear, their only objective was to give God praise.

Why? Because God had already promised the victory, and ultrafidian faith believes it in radical terms!

What audacious faith…what ultrafidian faith….what God-pleasing faith!

How do I know this pleased God? That is exactly what the word of God records:

"*At the very moment they began to sing and give praise*, the LORD caused the armies of Ammon, Moab, and Mount Seir to start fighting among themselves. [23] The armies of Moab and Ammon turned against their allies from Mount Seir and killed every one of them. After they had destroyed the army of Seir, they began attacking each other. [24] So when the army of Judah arrived at the lookout point in the wilderness, all they saw were dead bodies lying on the ground as far as they could see. Not a single one of the enemy had escaped." (*emphasis mine)* 2 Chronicles 20:22-24 (NLT)

The people of Judah did nothing but trust God with ultrafidian faith and loud praise, and God did the rest.

11

ADD TO ULTRAFIDIAN FAITH, PRAISE!

If you want to please God, have "ultrafidian faith" added with audible praise and watch what happens. God moves in the midst of those who truly believe...and show it by having an "ultrafidian faith" that displays itself in a demonstrative way.

I truly believe praise is a powerful "ultrafidian faith" tool. You can even see this in the New Testament.

In Acts 16, the Bible shares the story of Paul and Silas. The story finds them stripped, severely flogged, thrown in prison, shackled, and heavily guarded.

They found themselves there because they were doing the work of the kingdom by sharing the gospel of Jesus Christ. In so doing, a girl is set free from demonic possession. The authorities were very angry about this, for the young girl brought her handlers much income, so they apprehended Paul and Silas and brought them before the authorities.

They were thrown into the inner part of the prison. Most would agree that it was the worst place to be. All of the sewer from the rest of the prisoners would make its way to the inner part of the prison. Prisoners surrounded them, and there is a good possibility that prisoners then exhibited behavior somewhat like prisoners do today. They probably cursed openly, exhibited violent and angry tempers, and were intolerant of everyone else, just like today. More than likely, they used their 'position' in the prison hierarchy to push the 'newbies' around.

Some that are in similar circumstances would complain, fret, worry, and wonder out loud whether serving God was worth it. Most constantly complain and would do anything except do what Paul and Silas did in this situation.

What did Paul and Silas do? In the midst of the problem, Paul and Silas did the unthinkable:

"Around midnight Paul and Silas were praying and singing hymns to God, and the other prisoners were listening. " Acts 16:25 (NLT)

Can you imagine what this did to the other prisoners? The crass and the criminal element knew exactly what had happened to Paul and Silas. They probably discerned that Paul and Silas were not criminals and did not deserve what they received. They had probably expected to hear their moans from the pain, their complaints because of the conditions, and their bitterness because of their situation.

Instead, they hear praise expressed to God. It must have moved those prisoners to hear that praise.

It certainly moved God! The Bible says,

" Suddenly, there was a massive earthquake, and the prison was shaken to its foundations. All the doors immediately flew open, and the chains of every prisoner fell off! "Acts 16:26 (NLT)

There is no biblical proof of this, but I believe God looked down from heaven into that dark, sewer-infested prison cell, and saw two of His children praising Him. They were not praising Him because of blessing, but praising Him in spite of pain. They were not singing due to joy, but praising Him in spite of the situation. Their praise was audible and powerful. God may have summoned the creatures of Revelations, and commanded them to look at Paul and Silas as they praised God, not in the midst of heaven's splendor, but in the inner sewer-infested prison cell. He could have called the angels from their work stations for a moment and asked them to see what His children, who were no doubt bleeding and bruised, were doing. That 'ultrafidian faith' must have caused all of heaven to come to attention and take notice.

Maybe not, but this audible demonstration of faith and genuine worship of God shook the very foundations of the prison. I do not know if the scene in heaven was as I portrayed, but one thing had to be true: The heart of God was moved by their faith, and that shook the core of the foundations of their problems.

The same is true for us. The faith God calls us to express is audacious and radical. It is counterintuitive to the way people think. It is so powerful that God delights in us as we exhibit that 'ultrafidian faith' in our life, and even more powerfully moved when we praise Him before the answer comes.

Look at virtually every miracle and you will see more than a 'belief' kind of faith, but a faith that screams "you are God and I am putting radical and complete trust in you despite my circumstances".

That will illicit more than a casual word of 'nice faith', or 'thanks for the belief, buddy,' but will instead be the smooth and powerful words Jesus spoke to the Canaanite woman in Matthew 15:

"Dear woman," ... "your faith is great. Your request is granted." Your daughter is healed!" Matthew 15:28 (NLT)

Christ does not express these words in response to praying a certain way, or demonstrating actions in a formulized, linear process...it is in putting your faith in Jesus and then doing what He says. It is in expressing an ultrafidian faith in Christ, then watching Him do the incredible. It is following up with great praise.

When God says nothing, that silence does not mean He is mad or done with you. It may simply mean it is time to believe Him with an 'ultrafidian faith' that surpasses your mere belief and demonstrates itself by your actions and your praise.

Every situation is different. However, "When God Says Nothing" you can hear from God by doing the following:

1. Praying (not only the key in this book, but vital to your daily walk)

2. Ensuring that all sin has been confessed to God

3. Listening and obeying God (in every area and through all means described in the Bible)

4. Disregarding all distractions (players to prayers…people or otherwise)

5. Looking for ways to demonstrate an ultrafidian, audacious, bold, and daring faith to God.

6. Trusting God for the outcome.

7. Praising God regardless of circumstances!

12

FINAL WORDS

For the Canaanite woman, her final words were "Your faith is great, your daughter is whole." These are great "final words" for a person of ultrafidian faith.

But there is more to the faith walk than this. The follow-up of some of the "final words" given by Christ are as powerful as the "final words" He spoke.

In John 4, the Bible records this story:

"As he traveled through Galilee, he came to Cana, where he had turned the water into wine. There was a government official in nearby Capernaum whose son was very sick. [47] When he heard that Jesus had come from Judea to Galilee, he went and begged Jesus to come to Capernaum to heal his son, who was about to die. Jesus asked, "Will you never believe in me unless you see miraculous signs and wonders?" The official pleaded, "Lord, please come now before my little boy dies." Then Jesus told him, "Go back home. Your son will live!" And

the man believed what Jesus said and started home."
John 4:46-50 (NLT)

Great final words, "Your son will live!". But what
happens after the words are spoken helps us to
understand the effects of all that Christ wants to
accomplish through our problem. You may see a need
that only Christ can meet, and watch as Jesus responds
to your ultrafidian faith. After that, His objective is
more clear.

As in the story above, the man believed what Jesus
said, and started home. That was faith. He believed
and went home. His faith demanded action, and it
was to believe and go home. He went home...and this
is what the word of God says....

" While the man was on his way, some of his
servants met him with the news that his son was alive
and well. He asked them when the boy had begun to get
better, and they replied, "Yesterday afternoon at one
o'clock his fever suddenly disappeared!" Then the father
realized that that was the very time Jesus had told him,
"Your son will live." And he and his entire household
believed in Jesus." John 4:51-54 (NLT)

The final "word" in this passage was that the man and his entire household believed. The objective and aim of Christ is not just to meet a need, or to answer a prayer, but that you would express faith and trust in Him, showing an ultrafidian faith with added praise. The result then is that He alone gets the glory from what has occurred.

That should be our final aim. God gets the glory, and the expression of faith causes others to come to know the God that made it happen.

That is the best final word in any miracle.

Here are some final questions for you to consider:

1. What prayer have you prayed that God has not answered?

2. While you read this book, were there things that revealed possible reasons you were not getting an answer (sin, failing to forgive someone, etc.)?

3. Are there players to your prayers right now?

4. Are they positive (friends carrying the paralytic) or negative ("send her away, she is bothering us")?

5. What ways can you demonstrate ultrafidian faith?

6. What can you praise God for, right now, in spite of unanswered prayer?

7. What ways can God get great glory through a miracle He provides?

13

DO YOU HAVE A RELATIONSHIP WITH GOD?

This is the most important question in human existence and one whose answer is clearly outlined in scripture. In order to be saved, we must: realize how much God loves us, how sinful we are, and know that He alone can save us, cleanse us, and give us eternal life. Scripture tells us that Jesus is the **only** way and we cannot have access to God through **any** other means. In fact, in John 14:6, Jesus plainly stated,

"I am the way, the truth, and the life: no man comes to the Father, but by me." (NIV)

God Loves You!

God loves you so much that he made a way for you, through the shed blood of his son so that you might be able to spend eternity with Him.

"For God loved the world so much that he gave his one and only Son, so that everyone who believes in him will not perish but have eternal life. John 3:16 (NLT)

Man is a sinner, and sin has separated him from God!

You may think you are a good person but being good is not enough! Every man has sinned and there is none that is righteous before God!

"Not a single person on earth is always good and never sins." Eccl 7:20 (NLT)

"For everyone has sinned; we all fall short of God's glorious standard." Romans 3:23 (NLT)

Jesus Christ is the Only Answer for Sin!

Jesus Christ is the only remedy for sin. We cannot be good enough to get into heaven, nor can our good works get us there. There was no other way for God to erase the effect of sin except by blood. The shedding of Christ's blood indicated that the penalty for sin had been paid; a perfect sinless life had been sacrificed for the lives of all who have sinned.

". . . For without the shedding of blood, there is no forgiveness. Hebrews 9:22 (NLT)

"Christ suffered for our sins once for all time. He never sinned, but he died for sinners to bring you safely home to God." I Peter 3:18 (NLT)

"There is salvation in no one else! God has given no other name under heaven by which we must be saved." Acts 4:12 (NLT)

You Must Receive Jesus Christ as Your Lord and Savior!

To be saved, you must confess that Jesus is Lord, while acknowledging in his heart that Christ must have full rule over his life. This confession of Christ as Lord assumes that it is Christ who will work and fulfill His own righteousness within man, as man is unable to attain righteousness of his own accord.

Jesus calls this experience the "**new birth**." He told Nicodemus:

"... unless you are born again, you cannot see the Kingdom of God." John 3:3 (NLT)

We invite you now to receive the Lord Jesus Christ as your personal Savior.

"But to all who believed him and accepted him, he gave the right to become children of God." John 1:12 (NLT)

Pray this Prayer and Mean it with all Your Heart!

Dear Lord Jesus, I realize that I am a sinner and have broken your laws. I understand that my sin has separated me from you. I am sorry and I ask you to forgive me. I accept the fact that your son Jesus Christ died for me, was resurrected, is alive today, and hears my prayer. I now open my heart's door and invite Jesus in to become **my** Lord and **my** Savior. I give Him control and ask that He would rule and reign in my heart so that His perfect will would be accomplished in my life. In Jesus' name I pray. Amen.

Congratulations!

If you prayed this prayer in all sincerity, you are now a Child of God. However there are a few things that you need to do to follow up on your commitment.

- Get baptized (full immersion) in water as commanded by Christ.

- Tell someone else about your new faith in Christ.

- Spend time with God each day through prayer and Bible reading.

- Seek fellowship with other followers of Jesus at a Bible believing church.

Want to write the author and let him know of your commitment to follow Christ?

Write to him at the following address:

John Utley
P.O. Box 840
Granger, IN 46530

He will send you a book in the mail to help you as you begin your walk with Christ.

For more information on the author, or more resources, go to:
www.whenGodsaysnothing.com

14

QUESTIONS FOR YOUR FAITH JOURNEY!

Chapter 1~Praying Fervently!

1. What are the greatest prayers you have prayed that God has not answered?

2. Describe what faith is to you:

3. Write down prayers that God has answered:

    a. When God has said, "yes"

    b. When God said, "no"

c. When God said, "wait"

Complete the following sentence:

I feel _____

when God does not answer my prayer immediately.

Chapter 2~The God Who Hears

1. Have you ever felt that God was not even listening to your prayers?

2. Is it possible that some areas of your life are keeping you from an answered prayer (sin, unforgiveness, etc.)?

3. The author wrote, "When we walk the godly walk, we can rest assured God hears the godly talk" How does that statement affect your view of prayer?

Chapter 3~No One Is Paying Attention

1. Some people believe sincerity is enough to cause God to hear us. Do you agree or disagree? Explain.

2. Do you believe you have the capacity to pray "Elijah-like" prayers? Why or why not?

3. The author said, "The first key to those times when God says nothing is to KNOW that God hears you when you pray." Do you believe God hears you when you pray? If so, how does that help you pray more effectively?

Chapter 4~The players in our prayers

1. Who or what are the players to your prayers right now?

2. Who can you count on to pray for you, and offer positive support while you are praying for a need?

3. Is there a detractor (one that tries to cause you to doubt instead of believe God)?

4. How do you feel when people try to play a part in your prayer need?

5. Are the "players to your prayers" mainly well-meaning, self-seeking or malicious?

6. The author shared the story of the four men who brought their paralytic friend to Jesus. He shared that sometimes barriers may keep us from the Lord (such as pride or jealousy, past hurts, unforgiveness or sin). Do you feel that there are those barriers that keep you from the Lord?

If so, what can you do to get past these barriers?

7. The author discussed the roof, and called it a lid, keeping these men and their friend from their God-intended potential. These are limits and zones beyond our

comfort. Do you have lids that keep you from your full potential in prayer? If so, what are they?

Chapter 5~When God Speaks

1. How has God spoken to you in the past, as you have read the Bible?

2. The author shared that people think faster than people speak, and sometimes can anticipate what is being said. Have you noticed times when you have thought faster than someone spoke and misjudged what they said?

3. The author mentioned that God sometimes speaks through other people and offered a warning. Have you ever had someone say something to you that confirmed what God had already spoken?

4. The story of the young prophet and the old prophet the author shared stands as a warning to all to ensure that obedience to God is foremost. What can you do to ensure that you are hearing from God, and that you obey His directives?

5. The author shared the statement, "The Spirit and the Word always agree." Do you believe it is important to have that mindset? If so, why is it important?

Chapter 6~Jesus cares, He's just not concerned

1. The author shared that Jesus cared, but was not "concerned." That word "concerned" carries the thought of being worried. Do you believe God "worries" about something? Why or why not?

2. In your opinion, is it human nature to try to exaggerate our need to God in prayer to try to get Him to move quicker for us?

3. What is the danger of focusing on the need you have?

Chapter 7~Some storms are blessings!

1. The author said, "not every "storm" is a curse, and not every "blessing" is from the Lord" when he was talking about perspectives to the problem. What "storms" in your life turned out to be blessings....and what "blessings" turned out to be trap from the enemy?

2. Perspective is important. Is it an easy or difficult to look at your problem as an opportunity for God to show Himself powerful?

Chapter 8~ Beware of the comparison trap

1. Have you ever compared your problem to someone else's provision?

2. If so, how did that comparison affect your faith?

3. What is the best perspective to have when you are suffering and others are being blessed?

Chapter 9~The Right Response

1. The author shared that the Canaanite woman just wanted a crumb that fell from the children's table. Why do you think that the perspective of a "crumb" instead of a "big miracle" demonstrated her faith?

2. According to the author, what is the ONE thing that will please God?

Chapter 10~What Kind of Faith Is This

1. The author shared a faith that "laughs at calamity, balks at uncertainty, and looks at the storm as an opportunity for God to do the incredible." What would it take for you to have that kind of faith?

2. The word, "Ultrafidian" may be a new term for you. How does the author's description of this type of faith compare to the description of "faith" you have had in the past?

3. What needs to change in your mindset, your attitude and your walk with God in order to demonstrate "ultrafidian faith"?

Chapter 11~Add to Ultrafidian Faith, Praise!

1. Have you ever praised God for something He had not done yet (in faith, believing)?

2. How can you demonstrate "Ultrafidian Faith" to God in your situation today, and how can your praise add to that demonstration?

3. What are bold, daring ways you can praise God in the midst of unanswered prayer?

Chapter 12~Final Words

1. The author shared that the final word, after God has spoken, and performed the miracle, the final word from us should be to give God the glory. In what way could God get glory once the prayer is answered?

2. In what way(s) could God get glory today, even before the miracle has occurred?

Use this tool to help you as you seek God. Complete the left
column by indicating the prayer need you are committing to
God. In the right column, record how God answered your prayer
(could be "yes", could be "no", could be "wait", and could be a
miracle). Use additional sheets if necessary.

Prayers I have prayed	How God answered

Use this tool as you consider your request. How can you praise God while you are in the midst of the problem? In the left column, record what you can give God praise for, even before the prayer is answered. In the right column, record ways that you can demonstrate ultrafidian faith in your circumstance (could be the left and right columns show identical entries)

Things I can praise God for	How I can demonstrate ultrafidian faith